This chore chart belongs to

____

Morning Chores	S	M	T	W	T	F	S
Make Bed							
Go Potty							
Eat Breakfast							
Do your breakfast dishes							
Brush Teeth							
Get dressed							
PJs in hamper							
Socks and Shoes							
Backpack and Lunch bag							

Weekly Chores

Evening Chores	S	M	T	W	T	F	S
Put backpack away							
Eat Dinner							
Do your dinner dishes							
Put your toys away							
Bath or Shower							
PJ on							
Brush Teeth							
Go Potty							
Read a book							

Weekly Chores

	S	M	T	W	T	F	S

Morning Chores	S	M	T	W	T	F	S
Make Bed							
Go Potty							
Eat Breakfast							
Do your breakfast dishes							
Brush Teeth							
Get dressed							
PJs in hamper							
Socks and Shoes							
Backpack and Lunch bag							

Weekly Chores

Evening Chores	S	M	T	W	T	F	S
Put backpack away							
Eat Dinner							
Do your dinner dishes							
Put your toys away							
Bath or Shower							
PJ on							
Brush Teeth							
Go Potty							
Read a book							

Weekly Chores

	S	M	T	W	T	F	S

Morning Chores	S	M	T	W	T	F	S
Make Bed							
Go Potty							
Eat Breakfast							
Do your breakfast dishes							
Brush Teeth							
Get dressed							
PJs in hamper							
Socks and Shoes							
Backpack and Lunch bag							

Weekly Chores

Evening Chores

Evening Chores	S	M	T	W	T	F	S
Put backpack away							
Eat Dinner							
Do your dinner dishes							
Put your toys away							
Bath or Shower							
PJ on							
Brush Teeth							
Go Potty							
Read a book							

Weekly Chores

Morning Chores	S	M	T	W	T	F	S
Make Bed							
Go Potty							
Eat Breakfast							
Do your breakfast dishes							
Brush Teeth							
Get dressed							
PJs in hamper							
Socks and Shoes							
Backpack and Lunch bag							

Weekly Chores

Evening Chores	S	M	T	W	T	F	S
Put backpack away							
Eat Dinner							
Do your dinner dishes							
Put your toys away							
Bath or Shower							
PJ on							
Brush Teeth							
Go Potty							
Read a book							

Weekly Chores

Morning Chores	S	M	T	W	T	F	S
Make Bed							
Go Potty							
Eat Breakfast							
Do your breakfast dishes							
Brush Teeth							
Get dressed							
PJs in hamper							
Socks and Shoes							
Backpack and Lunch bag							

Weekly Chores

Evening Chores	S	M	T	W	T	F	S
Put backpack away							
Eat Dinner							
Do your dinner dishes							
Put your toys away							
Bath or Shower							
PJ on							
Brush Teeth							
Go Potty							
Read a book							

Weekly Chores

Morning Chores	S	M	T	W	T	F	S
Make Bed							
Go Potty							
Eat Breakfast							
Do your breakfast dishes							
Brush Teeth							
Get dressed							
PJs in hamper							
Socks and Shoes							
Backpack and Lunch bag							

Weekly Chores

Evening Chores	S	M	T	W	T	F	S
Put backpack away							
Eat Dinner							
Do your dinner dishes							
Put your toys away							
Bath or Shower							
PJ on							
Brush Teeth							
Go Potty							
Read a book							

Weekly Chores

	S	M	T	W	T	F	S

Morning Chores	S	M	T	W	T	F	S
Make Bed							
Go Potty							
Eat Breakfast							
Do your breakfast dishes							
Brush Teeth							
Get dressed							
PJs in hamper							
Socks and Shoes							
Backpack and Lunch bag							

Weekly Chores

Evening Chores	S	M	T	W	T	F	S
Put backpack away							
Eat Dinner							
Do your dinner dishes							
Put your toys away							
Bath or Shower							
PJ on							
Brush Teeth							
Go Potty							
Read a book							

Weekly Chores

	S	M	T	W	T	F	S

Morning Chores	S	M	T	W	T	F	S
Make Bed							
Go Potty							
Eat Breakfast							
Do your breakfast dishes							
Brush Teeth							
Get dressed							
PJs in hamper							
Socks and Shoes							
Backpack and Lunch bag							

Weekly Chores

Evening Chores	S	M	T	W	T	F	S
Put backpack away							
Eat Dinner							
Do your dinner dishes							
Put your toys away							
Bath or Shower							
PJ on							
Brush Teeth							
Go Potty							
Read a book							

Weekly Chores

	S	M	T	W	T	F	S

Morning Chores	S	M	T	W	T	F	S
Make Bed							
Go Potty							
Eat Breakfast							
Do your breakfast dishes							
Brush Teeth							
Get dressed							
PJs in hamper							
Socks and Shoes							
Backpack and Lunch bag							

Weekly Chores

Evening Chores	S	M	T	W	T	F	S
Put backpack away							
Eat Dinner							
Do your dinner dishes							
Put your toys away							
Bath or Shower							
PJ on							
Brush Teeth							
Go Potty							
Read a book							

Weekly Chores

Morning Chores	S	M	T	W	T	F	S
Make Bed							
Go Potty							
Eat Breakfast							
Do your breakfast dishes							
Brush Teeth							
Get dressed							
PJs in hamper							
Socks and Shoes							
Backpack and Lunch bag							

Weekly Chores

Evening Chores	S	M	T	W	T	F	S
Put backpack away							
Eat Dinner							
Do your dinner dishes							
Put your toys away							
Bath or Shower							
PJ on							
Brush Teeth							
Go Potty							
Read a book							

Weekly Chores

Morning Chores	S	M	T	W	T	F	S
Make Bed							
Go Potty							
Eat Breakfast							
Do your breakfast dishes							
Brush Teeth							
Get dressed							
PJs in hamper							
Socks and Shoes							
Backpack and Lunch bag							

Weekly Chores

Evening Chores	S	M	T	W	T	F	S
Put backpack away							
Eat Dinner							
Do your dinner dishes							
Put your toys away							
Bath or Shower							
PJ on							
Brush Teeth							
Go Potty							
Read a book							

Weekly Chores

Morning Chores	S	M	T	W	T	F	S
Make Bed							
Go Potty							
Eat Breakfast							
Do your breakfast dishes							
Brush Teeth							
Get dressed							
PJs in hamper							
Socks and Shoes							
Backpack and Lunch bag							

Weekly Chores

Evening Chores	S	M	T	W	T	F	S
Put backpack away							
Eat Dinner							
Do your dinner dishes							
Put your toys away							
Bath or Shower							
PJ on							
Brush Teeth							
Go Potty							
Read a book							

Weekly Chores

Morning Chores	S	M	T	W	T	F	S
Make Bed							
Go Potty							
Eat Breakfast							
Do your breakfast dishes							
Brush Teeth							
Get dressed							
PJs in hamper							
Socks and Shoes							
Backpack and Lunch bag							

Weekly Chores

Evening Chores	S	M	T	W	T	F	S
Put backpack away							
Eat Dinner							
Do your dinner dishes							
Put your toys away							
Bath or Shower							
PJ on							
Brush Teeth							
Go Potty							
Read a book							

Weekly Chores

Morning Chores	S	M	T	W	T	F	S
Make Bed							
Go Potty							
Eat Breakfast							
Do your breakfast dishes							
Brush Teeth							
Get dressed							
PJs in hamper							
Socks and Shoes							
Backpack and Lunch bag							

Weekly Chores

Evening Chores	S	M	T	W	T	F	S
Put backpack away							
Eat Dinner							
Do your dinner dishes							
Put your toys away							
Bath or Shower							
PJ on							
Brush Teeth							
Go Potty							
Read a book							

Weekly Chores

Morning Chores	S	M	T	W	T	F	S
Make Bed							
Go Potty							
Eat Breakfast							
Do your breakfast dishes							
Brush Teeth							
Get dressed							
PJs in hamper							
Socks and Shoes							
Backpack and Lunch bag							

Weekly Chores

Evening Chores

Evening Chores	S	M	T	W	T	F	S
Put backpack away							
Eat Dinner							
Do your dinner dishes							
Put your toys away							
Bath or Shower							
PJ on							
Brush Teeth							
Go Potty							
Read a book							

Weekly Chores

	S	M	T	W	T	F	S

Morning Chores	S	M	T	W	T	F	S
Make Bed							
Go Potty							
Eat Breakfast							
Do your breakfast dishes							
Brush Teeth							
Get dressed							
PJs in hamper							
Socks and Shoes							
Backpack and Lunch bag							

Weekly Chores

Evening Chores	S	M	T	W	T	F	S
Put backpack away							
Eat Dinner							
Do your dinner dishes							
Put your toys away							
Bath or Shower							
PJ on							
Brush Teeth							
Go Potty							
Read a book							

Weekly Chores

Morning Chores	S	M	T	W	T	F	S
Make Bed							
Go Potty							
Eat Breakfast							
Do your breakfast dishes							
Brush Teeth							
Get dressed							
PJs in hamper							
Socks and Shoes							
Backpack and Lunch bag							

Weekly Chores

Evening Chores	S	M	T	W	T	F	S
Put backpack away							
Eat Dinner							
Do your dinner dishes							
Put your toys away							
Bath or Shower							
PJ on							
Brush Teeth							
Go Potty							
Read a book							

Weekly Chores

Morning Chores	S	M	T	W	T	F	S
Make Bed							
Go Potty							
Eat Breakfast							
Do your breakfast dishes							
Brush Teeth							
Get dressed							
PJs in hamper							
Socks and Shoes							
Backpack and Lunch bag							

Weekly Chores

Evening Chores	S	M	T	W	T	F	S
Put backpack away							
Eat Dinner							
Do your dinner dishes							
Put your toys away							
Bath or Shower							
PJ on							
Brush Teeth							
Go Potty							
Read a book							

Weekly Chores

Morning Chores	S	M	T	W	T	F	S
Make Bed							
Go Potty							
Eat Breakfast							
Do your breakfast dishes							
Brush Teeth							
Get dressed							
PJs in hamper							
Socks and Shoes							
Backpack and Lunch bag							

Weekly Chores

Evening Chores	S	M	T	W	T	F	S
Put backpack away							
Eat Dinner							
Do your dinner dishes							
Put your toys away							
Bath or Shower							
PJ on							
Brush Teeth							
Go Potty							
Read a book							

Weekly Chores

Morning Chores	S	M	T	W	T	F	S
Make Bed							
Go Potty							
Eat Breakfast							
Do your breakfast dishes							
Brush Teeth							
Get dressed							
PJs in hamper							
Socks and Shoes							
Backpack and Lunch bag							

Weekly Chores

Evening Chores	S	M	T	W	T	F	S
Put backpack away							
Eat Dinner							
Do your dinner dishes							
Put your toys away							
Bath or Shower							
PJ on							
Brush Teeth							
Go Potty							
Read a book							

Weekly Chores

Morning Chores	S	M	T	W	T	F	S
Make Bed							
Go Potty							
Eat Breakfast							
Do your breakfast dishes							
Brush Teeth							
Get dressed							
PJs in hamper							
Socks and Shoes							
Backpack and Lunch bag							

Weekly Chores

Evening Chores	S	M	T	W	T	F	S
Put backpack away							
Eat Dinner							
Do your dinner dishes							
Put your toys away							
Bath or Shower							
PJ on							
Brush Teeth							
Go Potty							
Read a book							

Weekly Chores

Morning Chores	S	M	T	W	T	F	S
Make Bed							
Go Potty							
Eat Breakfast							
Do your breakfast dishes							
Brush Teeth							
Get dressed							
PJs in hamper							
Socks and Shoes							
Backpack and Lunch bag							

Weekly Chores

Evening Chores	S	M	T	W	T	F	S
Put backpack away							
Eat Dinner							
Do your dinner dishes							
Put your toys away							
Bath or Shower							
PJ on							
Brush Teeth							
Go Potty							
Read a book							

Weekly Chores

	S	M	T	W	T	F	S

Morning Chores	S	M	T	W	T	F	S
Make Bed							
Go Potty							
Eat Breakfast							
Do your breakfast dishes							
Brush Teeth							
Get dressed							
PJs in hamper							
Socks and Shoes							
Backpack and Lunch bag							

Weekly Chores

Evening Chores	S	M	T	W	T	F	S
Put backpack away							
Eat Dinner							
Do your dinner dishes							
Put your toys away							
Bath or Shower							
PJ on							
Brush Teeth							
Go Potty							
Read a book							

Weekly Chores

Morning Chores	S	M	T	W	T	F	S
Make Bed							
Go Potty							
Eat Breakfast							
Do your breakfast dishes							
Brush Teeth							
Get dressed							
PJs in hamper							
Socks and Shoes							
Backpack and Lunch bag							

Weekly Chores

	S	M	T	W	T	F	S

Evening Chores	S	M	T	W	T	F	S
Put backpack away							
Eat Dinner							
Do your dinner dishes							
Put your toys away							
Bath or Shower							
PJ on							
Brush Teeth							
Go Potty							
Read a book							

Weekly Chores

Morning Chores	S	M	T	W	T	F	S
Make Bed							
Go Potty							
Eat Breakfast							
Do your breakfast dishes							
Brush Teeth							
Get dressed							
PJs in hamper							
Socks and Shoes							
Backpack and Lunch bag							

Weekly Chores

Evening Chores	S	M	T	W	T	F	S
Put backpack away							
Eat Dinner							
Do your dinner dishes							
Put your toys away							
Bath or Shower							
PJ on							
Brush Teeth							
Go Potty							
Read a book							

Weekly Chores

Morning Chores	S	M	T	W	T	F	S
Make Bed							
Go Potty							
Eat Breakfast							
Do your breakfast dishes							
Brush Teeth							
Get dressed							
PJs in hamper							
Socks and Shoes							
Backpack and Lunch bag							

Weekly Chores

Evening Chores	S	M	T	W	T	F	S
Put backpack away							
Eat Dinner							
Do your dinner dishes							
Put your toys away							
Bath or Shower							
PJ on							
Brush Teeth							
Go Potty							
Read a book							

Weekly Chores

	S	M	T	W	T	F	S

Morning Chores	S	M	T	W	T	F	S
Make Bed							
Go Potty							
Eat Breakfast							
Do your breakfast dishes							
Brush Teeth							
Get dressed							
PJs in hamper							
Socks and Shoes							
Backpack and Lunch bag							

Weekly Chores

Evening Chores	S	M	T	W	T	F	S
Put backpack away							
Eat Dinner							
Do your dinner dishes							
Put your toys away							
Bath or Shower							
PJ on							
Brush Teeth							
Go Potty							
Read a book							

Weekly Chores

Morning Chores	S	M	T	W	T	F	S
Make Bed							
Go Potty							
Eat Breakfast							
Do your breakfast dishes							
Brush Teeth							
Get dressed							
PJs in hamper							
Socks and Shoes							
Backpack and Lunch bag							

Weekly Chores

Evening Chores	S	M	T	W	T	F	S
Put backpack away							
Eat Dinner							
Do your dinner dishes							
Put your toys away							
Bath or Shower							
PJ on							
Brush Teeth							
Go Potty							
Read a book							

Weekly Chores

	S	M	T	W	T	F	S

Morning Chores	S	M	T	W	T	F	S
Make Bed							
Go Potty							
Eat Breakfast							
Do your breakfast dishes							
Brush Teeth							
Get dressed							
PJs in hamper							
Socks and Shoes							
Backpack and Lunch bag							

Weekly Chores

Evening Chores	S	M	T	W	T	F	S
Put backpack away							
Eat Dinner							
Do your dinner dishes							
Put your toys away							
Bath or Shower							
PJ on							
Brush Teeth							
Go Potty							
Read a book							

Weekly Chores

Morning Chores	S	M	T	W	T	F	S
Make Bed							
Go Potty							
Eat Breakfast							
Do your breakfast dishes							
Brush Teeth							
Get dressed							
PJs in hamper							
Socks and Shoes							
Backpack and Lunch bag							

Weekly Chores

Evening Chores	S	M	T	W	T	F	S
Put backpack away							
Eat Dinner							
Do your dinner dishes							
Put your toys away							
Bath or Shower							
PJ on							
Brush Teeth							
Go Potty							
Read a book							

Weekly Chores

	S	M	T	W	T	F	S

Morning Chores	S	M	T	W	T	F	S
Make Bed							
Go Potty							
Eat Breakfast							
Do your breakfast dishes							
Brush Teeth							
Get dressed							
PJs in hamper							
Socks and Shoes							
Backpack and Lunch bag							

Weekly Chores

Evening Chores	S	M	T	W	T	F	S
Put backpack away							
Eat Dinner							
Do your dinner dishes							
Put your toys away							
Bath or Shower							
PJ on							
Brush Teeth							
Go Potty							
Read a book							

Weekly Chores

	S	M	T	W	T	F	S

Morning Chores	S	M	T	W	T	F	S
Make Bed							
Go Potty							
Eat Breakfast							
Do your breakfast dishes							
Brush Teeth							
Get dressed							
PJs in hamper							
Socks and Shoes							
Backpack and Lunch bag							

Weekly Chores

Evening Chores	S	M	T	W	T	F	S
Put backpack away							
Eat Dinner							
Do your dinner dishes							
Put your toys away							
Bath or Shower							
PJ on							
Brush Teeth							
Go Potty							
Read a book							

Weekly Chores

Morning Chores	S	M	T	W	T	F	S
Make Bed							
Go Potty							
Eat Breakfast							
Do your breakfast dishes							
Brush Teeth							
Get dressed							
PJs in hamper							
Socks and Shoes							
Backpack and Lunch bag							

Weekly Chores

Evening Chores	S	M	T	W	T	F	S
Put backpack away							
Eat Dinner							
Do your dinner dishes							
Put your toys away							
Bath or Shower							
PJ on							
Brush Teeth							
Go Potty							
Read a book							

Weekly Chores

Morning Chores	S	M	T	W	T	F	S
Make Bed							
Go Potty							
Eat Breakfast							
Do your breakfast dishes							
Brush Teeth							
Get dressed							
PJs in hamper							
Socks and Shoes							
Backpack and Lunch bag							

Weekly Chores

Evening Chores	S	M	T	W	T	F	S
Put backpack away							
Eat Dinner							
Do your dinner dishes							
Put your toys away							
Bath or Shower							
PJ on							
Brush Teeth							
Go Potty							
Read a book							

Weekly Chores

Morning Chores	S	M	T	W	T	F	S
Make Bed							
Go Potty							
Eat Breakfast							
Do your breakfast dishes							
Brush Teeth							
Get dressed							
PJs in hamper							
Socks and Shoes							
Backpack and Lunch bag							

Weekly Chores

Evening Chores	S	M	T	W	T	F	S
Put backpack away							
Eat Dinner							
Do your dinner dishes							
Put your toys away							
Bath or Shower							
PJ on							
Brush Teeth							
Go Potty							
Read a book							

Weekly Chores

	S	M	T	W	T	F	S

Morning Chores	S	M	T	W	T	F	S
Make Bed							
Go Potty							
Eat Breakfast							
Do your breakfast dishes							
Brush Teeth							
Get dressed							
PJs in hamper							
Socks and Shoes							
Backpack and Lunch bag							

Weekly Chores

Evening Chores	S	M	T	W	T	F	S
Put backpack away							
Eat Dinner							
Do your dinner dishes							
Put your toys away							
Bath or Shower							
PJ on							
Brush Teeth							
Go Potty							
Read a book							

Weekly Chores

	S	M	T	W	T	F	S

Morning Chores	S	M	T	W	T	F	S
Make Bed							
Go Potty							
Eat Breakfast							
Do your breakfast dishes							
Brush Teeth							
Get dressed							
PJs in hamper							
Socks and Shoes							
Backpack and Lunch bag							

Weekly Chores

Evening Chores	S	M	T	W	T	F	S
Put backpack away							
Eat Dinner							
Do your dinner dishes							
Put your toys away							
Bath or Shower							
PJ on							
Brush Teeth							
Go Potty							
Read a book							

Weekly Chores

Morning Chores	S	M	T	W	T	F	S
Make Bed							
Go Potty							
Eat Breakfast							
Do your breakfast dishes							
Brush Teeth							
Get dressed							
PJs in hamper							
Socks and Shoes							
Backpack and Lunch bag							

Weekly Chores

Evening Chores	S	M	T	W	T	F	S
Put backpack away							
Eat Dinner							
Do your dinner dishes							
Put your toys away							
Bath or Shower							
PJ on							
Brush Teeth							
Go Potty							
Read a book							

Weekly Chores

Morning Chores	S	M	T	W	T	F	S
Make Bed							
Go Potty							
Eat Breakfast							
Do your breakfast dishes							
Brush Teeth							
Get dressed							
PJs in hamper							
Socks and Shoes							
Backpack and Lunch bag							

Weekly Chores

Evening Chores	S	M	T	W	T	F	S
Put backpack away							
Eat Dinner							
Do your dinner dishes							
Put your toys away							
Bath or Shower							
PJ on							
Brush Teeth							
Go Potty							
Read a book							

Weekly Chores

Morning Chores	S	M	T	W	T	F	S
Make Bed							
Go Potty							
Eat Breakfast							
Do your breakfast dishes							
Brush Teeth							
Get dressed							
PJs in hamper							
Socks and Shoes							
Backpack and Lunch bag							

Weekly Chores

Evening Chores	S	M	T	W	T	F	S
Put backpack away							
Eat Dinner							
Do your dinner dishes							
Put your toys away							
Bath or Shower							
PJ on							
Brush Teeth							
Go Potty							
Read a book							

Weekly Chores

Morning Chores	S	M	T	W	T	F	S
Make Bed							
Go Potty							
Eat Breakfast							
Do your breakfast dishes							
Brush Teeth							
Get dressed							
PJs in hamper							
Socks and Shoes							
Backpack and Lunch bag							

Weekly Chores

Evening Chores	S	M	T	W	T	F	S
Put backpack away							
Eat Dinner							
Do your dinner dishes							
Put your toys away							
Bath or Shower							
PJ on							
Brush Teeth							
Go Potty							
Read a book							

Weekly Chores

	S	M	T	W	T	F	S

Morning Chores	S	M	T	W	T	F	S
Make Bed							
Go Potty							
Eat Breakfast							
Do your breakfast dishes							
Brush Teeth							
Get dressed							
PJs in hamper							
Socks and Shoes							
Backpack and Lunch bag							

Weekly Chores

Evening Chores	S	M	T	W	T	F	S
Put backpack away							
Eat Dinner							
Do your dinner dishes							
Put your toys away							
Bath or Shower							
PJ on							
Brush Teeth							
Go Potty							
Read a book							

Weekly Chores

Morning Chores	S	M	T	W	T	F	S
Make Bed							
Go Potty							
Eat Breakfast							
Do your breakfast dishes							
Brush Teeth							
Get dressed							
PJs in hamper							
Socks and Shoes							
Backpack and Lunch bag							

Weekly Chores

Evening Chores	S	M	T	W	T	F	S
Put backpack away							
Eat Dinner							
Do your dinner dishes							
Put your toys away							
Bath or Shower							
PJ on							
Brush Teeth							
Go Potty							
Read a book							

Weekly Chores

Morning Chores	S	M	T	W	T	F	S
Make Bed							
Go Potty							
Eat Breakfast							
Do your breakfast dishes							
Brush Teeth							
Get dressed							
PJs in hamper							
Socks and Shoes							
Backpack and Lunch bag							

Weekly Chores

Evening Chores	S	M	T	W	T	F	S
Put backpack away							
Eat Dinner							
Do your dinner dishes							
Put your toys away							
Bath or Shower							
PJ on							
Brush Teeth							
Go Potty							
Read a book							

Weekly Chores

	S	M	T	W	T	F	S

Morning Chores	S	M	T	W	T	F	S
Make Bed							
Go Potty							
Eat Breakfast							
Do your breakfast dishes							
Brush Teeth							
Get dressed							
PJs in hamper							
Socks and Shoes							
Backpack and Lunch bag							

Weekly Chores

Evening Chores	S	M	T	W	T	F	S
Put backpack away							
Eat Dinner							
Do your dinner dishes							
Put your toys away							
Bath or Shower							
PJ on							
Brush Teeth							
Go Potty							
Read a book							

Weekly Chores

	S	M	T	W	T	F	S

Morning Chores	S	M	T	W	T	F	S
Make Bed							
Go Potty							
Eat Breakfast							
Do your breakfast dishes							
Brush Teeth							
Get dressed							
PJs in hamper							
Socks and Shoes							
Backpack and Lunch bag							

Weekly Chores

Evening Chores	S	M	T	W	T	F	S
Put backpack away							
Eat Dinner							
Do your dinner dishes							
Put your toys away							
Bath or Shower							
PJ on							
Brush Teeth							
Go Potty							
Read a book							

Weekly Chores

	S	M	T	W	T	F	S

Morning Chores	S	M	T	W	T	F	S
Make Bed							
Go Potty							
Eat Breakfast							
Do your breakfast dishes							
Brush Teeth							
Get dressed							
PJs in hamper							
Socks and Shoes							
Backpack and Lunch bag							

Weekly Chores

Evening Chores	S	M	T	W	T	F	S
Put backpack away							
Eat Dinner							
Do your dinner dishes							
Put your toys away							
Bath or Shower							
PJ on							
Brush Teeth							
Go Potty							
Read a book							

Weekly Chores

Morning Chores	S	M	T	W	T	F	S
Make Bed							
Go Potty							
Eat Breakfast							
Do your breakfast dishes							
Brush Teeth							
Get dressed							
PJs in hamper							
Socks and Shoes							
Backpack and Lunch bag							

Weekly Chores

Evening Chores	S	M	T	W	T	F	S
Put backpack away							
Eat Dinner							
Do your dinner dishes							
Put your toys away							
Bath or Shower							
PJ on							
Brush Teeth							
Go Potty							
Read a book							

Weekly Chores

Morning Chores	S	M	T	W	T	F	S
Make Bed							
Go Potty							
Eat Breakfast							
Do your breakfast dishes							
Brush Teeth							
Get dressed							
PJs in hamper							
Socks and Shoes							
Backpack and Lunch bag							

Weekly Chores

Evening Chores	S	M	T	W	T	F	S
Put backpack away							
Eat Dinner							
Do your dinner dishes							
Put your toys away							
Bath or Shower							
PJ on							
Brush Teeth							
Go Potty							
Read a book							

Weekly Chores

	S	M	T	W	T	F	S

Morning Chores	S	M	T	W	T	F	S
Make Bed							
Go Potty							
Eat Breakfast							
Do your breakfast dishes							
Brush Teeth							
Get dressed							
PJs in hamper							
Socks and Shoes							
Backpack and Lunch bag							

Weekly Chores

Evening Chores	S	M	T	W	T	F	S
Put backpack away							
Eat Dinner							
Do your dinner dishes							
Put your toys away							
Bath or Shower							
PJ on							
Brush Teeth							
Go Potty							
Read a book							

Weekly Chores

Morning Chores	S	M	T	W	T	F	S
Make Bed							
Go Potty							
Eat Breakfast							
Do your breakfast dishes							
Brush Teeth							
Get dressed							
PJs in hamper							
Socks and Shoes							
Backpack and Lunch bag							

Weekly Chores

Evening Chores	S	M	T	W	T	F	S
Put backpack away							
Eat Dinner							
Do your dinner dishes							
Put your toys away							
Bath or Shower							
PJ on							
Brush Teeth							
Go Potty							
Read a book							

Weekly Chores

Morning Chores	S	M	T	W	T	F	S
Make Bed							
Go Potty							
Eat Breakfast							
Do your breakfast dishes							
Brush Teeth							
Get dressed							
PJs in hamper							
Socks and Shoes							
Backpack and Lunch bag							

Weekly Chores

	S	M	T	W	T	F	S

Evening Chores	S	M	T	W	T	F	S
Put backpack away							
Eat Dinner							
Do your dinner dishes							
Put your toys away							
Bath or Shower							
PJ on							
Brush Teeth							
Go Potty							
Read a book							

Weekly Chores

	S	M	T	W	T	F	S

Morning Chores	S	M	T	W	T	F	S
Make Bed							
Go Potty							
Eat Breakfast							
Do your breakfast dishes							
Brush Teeth							
Get dressed							
PJs in hamper							
Socks and Shoes							
Backpack and Lunch bag							

Weekly Chores

Evening Chores	S	M	T	W	T	F	S
Put backpack away							
Eat Dinner							
Do your dinner dishes							
Put your toys away							
Bath or Shower							
PJ on							
Brush Teeth							
Go Potty							
Read a book							

Weekly Chores

	S	M	T	W	T	F	S

Morning Chores	S	M	T	W	T	F	S
Make Bed							
Go Potty							
Eat Breakfast							
Do your breakfast dishes							
Brush Teeth							
Get dressed							
PJs in hamper							
Socks and Shoes							
Backpack and Lunch bag							

Weekly Chores

Evening Chores	S	M	T	W	T	F	S
Put backpack away							
Eat Dinner							
Do your dinner dishes							
Put your toys away							
Bath or Shower							
PJ on							
Brush Teeth							
Go Potty							
Read a book							

Weekly Chores

	S	M	T	W	T	F	S